Praise for books in the *It's OK* series

"This book deals sensitively with its subject . . . Now parents have a tool that they can use in teaching their kids. Especially important is the fact that the book helps get parents and children actively involved."

— Dr. Regina Pally, Chairman of the Women's Committee of the Southern California Psychiatric Society, Faculty member, UCLA

"This book is a superb tool for parents and educators to use in helping children to understand their emotions."

— National Kid Watch Program (1-800-KID WATCH)

Look for these other books in the *It's O.K.* series:

IT'S O.K. TO SAY NO!
SOMETIMES IT'S O.K. TO TELL SECRETS!
IT'S O.K. TO SAY NO TO DRUGS!
SOMETIMES IT'S O.K. TO BE ANGRY!
IT'S O.K. TO BE SHY!
SOMETIMES IT'S O.K. TO BE AFRAID!
IT'S O.K. TO BE DIFFERENT!

SOMETIMES IT'S O.K. TO BE AFRAID!

A PARENT/CHILD MANUAL FOR THE EDUCATION OF CHILDREN

Dr. Mitch Golant with Bob Crane

Illustrated by Frank C. Smith

TOR

A TOM DOHERTY ASSOCIATES BOOK

The stories in chapter five are works of fiction. All the characters and events portrayed in this chapter and in other examples in this book are fictional. Any resemblance to real people or incidents is purely coincidental.

SOMETIMES IT'S O.K. TO BE AFRAID!

First printing: March 1988

A TOR Book

Published by Tom Doherty Associates Inc.
49 West 24th Street
New York, NY 10010

Cover art by Frank C. Smith

ISBN: 0-812-59564-9
CAN. ED.: 0-812-59465-7

Printed in the United States of America

0 9 8 7 6 5 4 3 2 1

SOMETIMES IT'S O.K. TO BE AFRAID!

Introduction

Yes, it is O.K. to be afraid. In fact, having certain fears is actually smart. Consider the dangers we'd all encounter if fear weren't a natural part of the human makeup. Fire, knives, street traffic—these are some of the things that are meant to be treated with a dose of healthy respect. Unfortunately, many of us won't acknowledge our fears. We consider any such acknowledgments a sign of weakness.

This attitude has an undesirable impact on our children. Most children have fears of one kind or another. Children's feelings usually run deeper than adults', and are more mysterious to them. That is certainly true of fear. Children lack the experience and the maturity to understand their fears and acknowledge them for what they are—a natural part of living.

When they realize that many adults hide their fears, children begin to mask their own, assuming that to show fear is to be inadequate. Because we want our children to be healthy and happy and to feel good about themselves, we must encourage them to communicate their fears to us. We then have to find ways to help them understand these fears and to respond to them in an appropriate manner. The appropriate response, of course, differs in different situations. The fear of an advancing train is a feeling to be heeded, while the fear of new experiences may be overcome.

In any event, our children have to learn that being afraid is not something to be ashamed of and that fear is not necessarily something that limits them. Chilren need to believe that it's O.K. to be afraid.

Chapter 1

Why Don't I Remember My Own Childhood Fears?

As adults, we tend to forget the fears we had as children, and how deeply we felt them. Time often erodes all but the most dramatic experiences of our childhood. An example:

A father was having difficulty relating to his young daughter's fear of the dark. He didn't remember having experienced anything similar until his own mother reminded him of a particularly harrowing experience he had when he was only seven.

Early on a Saturday morning he set out, alone, for a church function. His route took him across an overpass spanning a highway. He saw a man lying on the sidewalk beside the overpass. The man was probably only a drifter, perhaps sleeping off a drunk, but the child concluded that this was a dead body.

A couple of hours later, returning from the function, the boy approached the other end of the overpass. But he couldn't cross. He so feared the possibility of seeing the "body" again that he became almost paralyzed. He sat on the sidewalk and cried. An hour went by and still he could not move.

Finally, a sympathetic policeman on patrol walked by and escorted him across the overpass. The "dead"

man was gone. But the experience affected the child for some time thereafter.

This story is illustrative for a variety of reasons. As adults, we necessarily become more rational in order to survive; we lose the extremism that marks the child's imagination. We learn that there really aren't monsters lurking under the bed, that the shadows on the wall will not jump off and attack us, and that the unusual house on the corner with all the overgrown weeds hiding the windows is neither haunted nor occupied by the Munsters. But in gradually learning these lessons, we often forget just how real and terrible childhood fears actually were.

When the man in the story remembered the incident, and the deep fear it provoked, he then had a common experience with his daughter and thus a feeling to share with her. If we can all remember what frightened us the most when we were young, then we can communicate these feelings to our children. Children often do not believe that their parents had problems similar to their own, and this important communication will establish closer bonding between them and their parents. At the same time, we can help our children understand that their fears do not have to be paralyzing, and will not last forever.

4

The fear response is very natural and human. Studies have determined that all children experience what amounts to fear, stress, or anxiety in response to a fairly predictable gamut of circumstances. For example, at about six months of age, when babies are just beginning to recognize faces, they often react fearfully to strangers. The intensity of that fear is determined by the proximity of a parent or other familiar and trusted person. If the baby is being held by mother or father when a stranger approaches, the infant may turn his or her face into the parent but otherwise exhibit relatively little fear. If, however, the baby is across the room from a parent, an approaching stranger will likely send the child scurrying for the comfort and shelter of the parent.

At about the age of eighteen months to two years, a predictable fear of loud noises develops. At ages two or three, a fear of the dark becomes common, and at three or four, children often feel a fear of animals. At five years of age or thereabouts, children become fearful of bodily harm, either to themselves or to a member of their family. This, in turn, develops into the so-called separation anxiety, a fear that a parent leaving the child for any length of time will not return. Children raised in one-parent families, because of either divorce or death, are particularly likely to experience this fear in its extreme, clinging to the remaining parent and begging not to be left. Gentle but firm reassurance is what these children need. The intensity and duration of any of these fears vary, depending on the child and the situation.

When children of any age show fear, it is important to remember that the fear is very real and not to be dismissed lightly. In addition to the fears mentioned above, which are experienced by most children, your child may develop a fear of a particular object or person. Any fear should be responded to in a sensitive and understanding way. If these childhood fears fail to extinguish themselves with time, it is possible that they will become phobias, but that is not the usual pattern. The frightening experience would have to be extremely traumatic in order to generate a phobia.

A good friend of mine has a son who, at age eight, began to exhibit absolute panic whenever an airplane flew overhead. Through a series of questions, his parents determined that what frightened him was the thought that the plane might fall and hurt him. The parents do not know what triggered this fear, and their reassurances and explanations have so far had little effect. They plan to seek professional counseling if the boy continues to be scared of airplanes, recognizing that there are times when even a parent's best efforts are not sufficient.

Another man I know has a daughter who refused to step on the cracks in the sidewalk while she walked. At first, her parents thought it was just a game she was playing; after all, this is something many children do. As the days passed and she still stepped over every crack, they grew agitated and demanded that she walk normally. She refused and began to cry and scream. Eventually, through questioning, her parents discovered that, while it had begun as a game, one of the older girls in school told her that if she were ever to step on a crack, her parents would die. In a child's mind, anything is possible, and she believed the malicious lie.

Slowly and gently, her parents were able to demonstrate that stepping on a crack in the sidewalk would not cause their demise.

On examination, children's fears are not too different from adult fears. To children, the world is a mystical, magical place where the demons in their imagination are given free rein. While most adults are no longer afraid of the boogeyman, the unknown still causes a lot of sleepless nights; what if such and such doesn't happen, we wonder to ourselves, or what if such and such does? Yet we go on with our lives, not allowing our fears to paralyze us.

There are as many individual fears as there are individuals. Different things elicit fear in different people, and we must not think less of anyone for displaying fear. It's what we do with fear, how we handle it, that's important. That's the lesson we have to teach our kids.

Chapter 2

What Can I Do When My Children Are Afraid?

The following stories are about five different children, suffering from five different fears. These examples are not unusual among children. In fact, they are cited because they are so very common.

Jimmy is six and the youngest of three children. He has two older sisters, aged eleven and nine. Until recently, his parents have never had any reason to worry about Jimmy.

In the past few months, Jimmy has developed a fear of the dark. He is reluctant to go to bed at night. Twice, his parents have heard him scream in the middle of the night. On both occasions, Jimmy ran to his parents' bedroom, trembling with fear.

Several times his mother and father have found lights on in Jimmy's room late at night, though Jimmy was asleep. Once when his mother went to awaken him in the morning, she discovered Jimmy sleeping under his bed.

Jimmy's parents are understandably disturbed by this behavior. They had no comparable experiences with their older daughters, so they don't know what to do about it. They have had conflicting advice from friends. Some say they should leave a night-light on in Jimmy's room. Others say they shouldn't, claiming that Jimmy will then never get over his fear of the dark.

Jimmy's case is not unusual. In fact, Jimmy's behavior can be said to be natural. He fears the dark, as does almost everyone to some extent. This is really a fear of the unknown.

Let's take a closer look at this situation. Jimmy's parents never saw any signs of fear of the dark in their daughters. However, when the girls were younger, the family lived in a smaller home, and they shared a bedroom. Having another person in the same room lessens a child's fear of the dark.

What is it that Jimmy specifically fears? Jimmy has a fear of intrusion by a person or "monster" intent on attacking him in the night. He does not recognize this fear as irrational, even though his father has reassured him over and over again that it is. Such comments will not comfort Jimmy until time and his own psychological growth help him to overcome his fear. The threat may be imaginary, but the fear is not.

In bed in the dark, Jimmy is overcome by his sense of powerlessness and by his fear of separation from his parents. These two factors provide clues to how Jimmy's parents can help him deal with his fear.

What can Jimmy's parents do? First, Jimmy needs comfort, and assurance that his parents are there to protect him. As a small child, Jimmy is powerless, and he knows it. In comforting Jimmy, his parents can attempt to substitute one imagined scenario for another. They can suggest to Jimmy that when he feels frightened at night he imagine that his parents are his giant protectors and that he picture himself in a safe place.

It might help Jimmy immensely if his parents installed a night-light in his dark bedroom. A light that he can control himself might be even more helpful. A small flashlight or easy access to a switch that turns on a bedroom light gives the child control over a potentially frightening situation. If the child is frightened, he or she can quickly switch on the light and the threat goes away. When the child repeats this action many times and finds no cause for alarm, the fear may begin to diminish.

A slightly different approach can also be helpful. Some fears can be overcome in a step-by-step fashion by slowly desensitizing the fearful child. This process requires identifying precisely what it is the child fears. In Jimmy's case, his parents might attempt to desensitize him to his fear of the dark by installing a light dimmer in his room. The dimmer can be set at first to whatever level Jimmy is most comfortable with. Over time, the amount of light can be slowly reduced. With each decrease in light, Jimmy's parents should make sure Jimmy is not frightened.

Parents sometimes believe that giving a child control over the lights in his or her bedroom will encourage late-night play. You can deal with that possibility by stressing to the child that control over the lights is

intended only to help him or her overcome a fear of the dark.

Children's imaginations are unbounded. That's normal. It's part of the childhood experience. In the dark, a jacket draped casually over the back of a chair can look like an intruder. The reflected headlights of passing cars can produce unfamiliar shadow patterns in a child's room. A stuffed animal placed in a new location becomes a threatening object once the lights are out. Whatever it is that causes a child's nighttime fear is essentially meaningless. In Jimmy's case, it is important that he be encouraged to specifically identify what he is imagining.

His parents can help to define his fear by encouraging Jimmy to enact from beginning to end the imaginary event that causes him to panic during the night. For example, after Jimmy's mother has comforted him and assured him that she and his father are always prepared to protect him, no matter what happens, she can say, "Jimmy, what did you think was happening?" Their conversation might proceed in this fashion:

JIMMY: I thought there was a big monster coming in the window.

MOTHER: A monster? What did he look like?

JIMMY: He was huge. All hairy and everything, and he had great big teeth.

MOTHER: That sounds scary, all right. I can see why you were afraid. What do you think the monster was going to do to you? Show me. Jimmy's mother places a pillow in the center of the bed.] Pretend this pillow is you, and that you're the monster.

With a little encouragement, Jimmy's mother can help him play out his imagined threat.

JIMMY: The monster comes through the window. Grrrr! Grrrr! He sees me on top of the bed. He comes over. Grrrr! Grrrr! He leaps on top of me. Pow! Wham! We wrestle. I try to fight him off . . .

Although Jimmy's flight of fancy may sound gruesome, the playacting, with all the details included, has therapeutic value. It gives him power over his fears.

There is no sense for the parent to keep a straight face if it's impossible. It's better to encourage the child than to suppress laughter.

MOTHER [laughing]:   Jimmy, that's fantastic. Keep it up.

By the time Jimmy has completed acting out the scenario in his imagination, he, too, may find it rather funny.

Jimmy's mother can also suggest that Jimmy make specific demands of the monster:

MOTHER: Jimmy, because this monster woke you up by scaring you, I think he ought to be punished. What should we do to him? Would you like to throw him in the dungeon or banish him to a desert island?

JIMMY: Lock him up forever and ever!

The mother can suggest that the next day Jimmy draw a picture of the monster or make a model of it in clay. In any event, before he is put back to bed, Jimmy needs more comforting and reassurance. A hug is exactly what he needs. His mother or father might say something to the effect that they knew he had a very bad scare and it's no wonder he was so frightened. "Remember, we're right down the hall," they say, "and protecting you is the most important thing in our lives. We want you to tell us anytime something frightens you."

It is important that Jimmy's parents remember that a child's fears are real and tangible to the child. It would not help Jimmy to attempt to convince him that what he fears is imaginary or that nothing really happened. In his mind, something did happen.

Shelley is a bright, inquisitive seven-year-old. She does very well in school and gets along nicely with her classmates and her neighborhood friends.

Shelley's mother was surprised to discover that Shelley has a fear that is almost numbing. The woman discovered this fear by chance. Shelley might never have said anything about it.

Shelley and her mother were walking toward the family car after shopping in a mall near their home. Shelley suddenly grabbed her mother's hand and squeezed it almost painfully hard. The child was visibly trembling. Her mother said to Shelley, "What's wrong?" Shelley did not reply.

Approaching mother and daughter was a man seated in a motorized wheelchair. Shelley's mother knew the man from the neighborhood. He had been stricken with polio as a child and lost the use of his legs. Obviously, Shelley suffered from a deep fear of this man, and because of his condition, she felt guilty about her reaction. Every time she saw him on the street, she literally panicked.

One Saturday afternoon Shelley and some friends were playing a game in the school yard. Their ball got loose and Shelley ran after it. She glanced up and saw the man in the wheelchair watching her from outside the fence. Shelley stopped in her tracks and then fled the school yard, her friends watching in confusion and dismay.

Such a fear is not uncommon in children. Shelley is afraid that whatever happened to the man could happen to her. It is what the man symbolizes, not the man himself, that poses the threat to Shelley and causes her panic. What can Shelley's mother do to help her cope with her fear?

First, Shelley needs to know that her fear is not unusual. That may help her feel less guilty and uncomfortable about reacting as she does. Second, she needs to understand the real nature of her fear. Third, she needs to learn more about the object of her fear, the man in the wheelchair.

One of Shelley's difficulties is that she doesn't understand her reaction, and because she doesn't see a similar reaction in her friends, she may assume that something is wrong with her.

Shelley's mother can explain to her that she reacts as she does because the man reminds Shelley that serious things can happen to us—things over which we have no control. It may help Shelley to know that her reaction may arise partly from a deep sympathy for the man, which has translated into a fear that she could suffer the same fate.

Her mother should also tell her of the cause of the man's condition, a tragic disease against which Shelley herself has been inoculated. That may reassure Shelley and ease her fears. Her mother can also explain that accidents can result in a similar handicap, helping her to recognize that fears are actually good for us.

Once Shelley understands her fear, she can begin the step-by-step process of desensitizing. Her mother can encourage her to work through her fear by not turning away when she sees the man on the street. Eventually, she may become comfortable enough to pass him on the street or even to say hello.

It is important for children to learn that they do not have to accommodate a fear, that they don't have to give in to it. Sometimes it is simply a matter of gathering up courage and pushing through the barrier of fear. Facing up to fear—understanding its source—is the strongest weapon a child has in the fight against it.

Eddie is eight and has a fear of electrical storms. Lightning and thunder put him into a panic. If he hears a storm approaching, he often will run to his bedroom, get under his bed, and pull a heavy blanket over his head so

16

that the lightning is not visible.

His parents weren't aware of this fear until they heard Eddie's eleven-year-old brother, Todd, taunting him about it. At that time, Eddie managed to convince his parents that Todd was exaggerating the depth of his reaction.

Eddie's parents came face-to-face with the extent of the boy's difficulty over dinner one evening. The summer day had been hot and muggy. As the family sat down to dinner, distant rumblings of thunder could be heard. Within ten minutes, a powerful thunderstorm hit. Eddie summoned all his resources and tried to hold himself together. It was useless. He shivered and broke out in a cold sweat. Finally, when he could stand it no more, he ran to his room.

How can Eddie's parents help him cope with his fear?

The thunderstorm Eddie fears is more tangible than Jimmy's dread of the dark or Shelley's fear of the man in the wheelchair. A thunderstorm can be frightening to anyone. It is one of nature's most awesome displays of power. Still, help can be found. Children's curiosity can be used to help them better understand the things they fear. Sharks fascinate children, as do snakes, predators, "monsters," and almost anything else that might be considered fearsome. As much as children are "grossed out" by these things, they are drawn to them. That compulsion is a strong stimulus to learning, if a parent offers suggestions and guidance. And information itself can often extinguish the fear.

Eddie would be helped if he had a clear understanding of what a thunderstorm is and what humans have done to protect themselves from the destructive aspects of lightning. Eddie may not be aware that the lightning rod on his home would harmlessly ground almost any lightning that struck the house. Eddie might also be helped if he can identify the precise cause of his fear. Is it the lightning or the thunder?

Once the source of his fear has been precisely identified, Eddie's parents can help him begin the process of desensitizing himself to his fear of thunderstorms. The first step would be for one or both parents to take Eddie to a safe place when a thunderstorm breaks out. A warm embrace and some comforting words will help Eddie through the ordeal.

Keep in mind that this would be an important first step for Eddie. He has been reacting to his fear by fleeing and hiding under his bed until the storm passes. The strength of parental presence in a safe environment will help Eddie overcome his desire to hide from the storm.

Step by step, his parents can move Eddie to other rooms in the house, where the sights and sounds of a storm may be increasingly evident. Keep in mind, however, that throughout this desensitizing process Eddie will need a parent's warmth, comfort, and reassurance.

Valerie is seven and suffers from a fear of heights that manifests itself in dizziness and sometimes nausea. She has been troubled by this condition for the past two years. Valerie first noticed her reaction to heights while climbing a playground slide with some friends. She almost toppled off the slide's ladder when she reached the top and looked down. Since then, she has avoided situations that place her in jeopardy.

Her parents became aware of her problem when the family visited New York and made a trip to the top of the Empire State Building. Valerie became sick when they reached the building's observation deck.

Her parents are concerned about Valerie's fear of

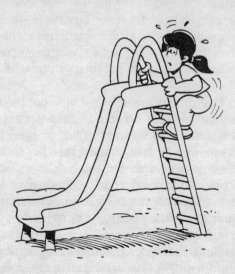

heights and don't know what to do about it. Valerie is bothered by it, too, because she doesn't understand her reaction and assumes that there is something wrong with her. Moreover, her friends tease her every time they play on an apparatus that Valerie can't climb.

Valerie's problem may be quite different from those of Jimmy, Shelley, and Eddie. Her fear of heights may have a physical basis, caused perhaps by abnormalities in the inner ear, the mechanism that governs the human sense of balance. Except in rare cases, such abnormalities in the inner ear are not caused by disease, but are inherited. Although they may affect the individual for a lifetime, some children who suffer from the fear of heights may literally grow out of it as the mechanism of the inner ear changes with maturity.

Valerie's parents would be well advised to consult a physician about her condition. Though the doctor may not be able to correct the condition, he or she should at least be able to identify it as physical rather than emotional. Proper diagnosis is important for Valerie's sake. If her fear has a physical cause that does not correct itself, she should avoid most circumstances that could make her feel ill. In some situations—airplane flights, for example—there are medicines that will provide relief for her symptoms. Awareness permits her to be prepared for such potentially stressful situations.

If, on the other hand, Valerie's fear is not physically induced, her parents may be able to help her gradually overcome her fear by desensitizing her to heights. For example, her mother or father could take her to a place around the house where there is a height with which Valerie is reasonably comfortable. Gradually, Valerie could be encouraged to reach for higher elevations. A parent's strong embrace would be particularly reassuring to Valerie in such a situation.

Keep in mind that desensitization is best attempted when the child expresses a desire and interest in over-

coming his or her fear. If the child is at all reluctant, nothing will be gained by forcing a confrontation with fear. Parents need to *encourage* a child to deal with his or her fear rather than *force* the child to do so. Force can lead to resentment, and with that resentment may come a stubborn refusal to learn, resulting in a diminished sense of self-esteem. A better tactic is to create an environment in which the child feels safe and protected, knowing he or she has unconditional love and support. Allow your child to feel O.K. about his or her fear.

Paul is seven and an "average" kid, according to his father. He loves sports and always seems to have a baseball glove or a soccer ball or a football helmet in his hands.

Last year, Paul's parents bought a summer house at the edge of a big lake in the mountains. It was something they had planned for since Paul was an infant. However, Paul's summer-long fearful reaction to the lake put a damper on his parents' enthusiasm for the new house.

Paul's apparent fear of the water came as a complete surprise to his parents. In anticipation of the move to the new summer house, Paul was given swimming lessons at the community pool in their hometown. He soon became an accomplished swimmer, and in fact won first prize in an age-group competition.

At the family's vacation home, Paul's confidence in his swimming ability seemed to vanish completely. All through the summer, he refused to venture more than a few feet from the lake's edge, and when the family went boating, Paul was clearly uneasy. The fact that Paul's five-year-old brother, David, took to the water like a fish only made matters worse.

Paul's parents were baffled. His reaction left them a little heartsick and mildly resentful. They had planned and saved for years for this second home, and they interpreted Paul's reaction as a rejection of everything they had worked for. What Paul's parents didn't understand was that Paul didn't really suffer from a fear of water. If it were water that he feared, he wouldn't have adapted so well to swimming in the community pool.

Paul fears the unknown aspects of the lake, and his sense of powerlessness over that unknown. The lake is deep and dark. For Paul, the lake's placid surface hides unseen terrors. Paul's parents incorrectly assumed that, because of his fear, Paul does not like the mountain retreat. That isn't the case. In fact, Paul is awed by the beauty of the place. He will sit on the deck in the evening and watch the sun go down over the lake, and his sense of contentment is almost palpable. What can Paul's parents do to help him?

First, they should not force him to confront his fear. Unfortunately, his father believes in the "sink or swim" theory of dealing with fear. He has suggested that Paul just jump into the deep water of the lake and swim his way out of his fear.

If Paul tried it, he might very well swim, since he has the ability, but he might sink psychologically. The experience could be so traumatic for him that he might never again set foot in the lake.

Paul's parents need to show Paul that they understand his fear. They can discuss some of the things that bother him about the lake—that he cannot see what is under the water, that he does not know how deep the lake is, that he does not know what kinds of fish live in the lake, or if they will bite. They can explain that everyone fears the unknown, and tell him that they are all going to learn more about the lake.

Paul's parents could help him by buying snorkeling gear for him and encouraging him to explore underwater life at the lake's edge. His explorations would probably boost Paul's confidence and ease his fears. As Paul becomes more confident of his understanding of marine life in the lake, he may become more venturesome in his aquatic activities.

Paul may also benefit from studying aquatic life in a book, learning more about what lives in the dark water. In the same vein, a family trip to an aquarium can be beneficial, both for the knowledge it imparts to Paul and for the sense of togetherness created on a family outing.

In this case, Paul's fear thrives, both literally and figuratively, in darkness; it was created out of ignorance. Knowledge dispels ignorance and is the most powerful tool human beings have for extinguishing the dark.

Chapter 3

What Do These Five Stories Tell Us About Dealing With Fear?

The first lesson we can learn from the experiences of the five children in Chapter Two is that the fear we see may be symbolic of a more comprehensive and deeper fear.

Jimmy feared the dark; Paul feared going into the water. The underlying fear in both cases was probably a dread of the unknown, combined with a sense of powerlessness. Shelley's fear of the man in the wheelchair was directed not at the man himself, but at what he symbolized. Valerie's fear of heights may have been a symptom of a physical problem.

Eddie's fear of thunderstorms comes closest to matching a fear and the object of that fear. But even there, a deeper psychological difficulty may have been at work. His underlying fear may be of things he cannot control. A thunderstorm is a dramatic example of something uncontrollable.

From a practical standpoint, you can help a child by first addressing the immediate object of his or her fear. If a child can begin to cope with the symbol, he will take an important step toward coping with the underlying fear. Let's use Paul as an example.

It may help Paul to understand that his fear of the water in the mountain lake is essentially a fear of the unknown. But that's not vitally important to him. The three steps that will be of greatest help to Paul are: first, to acknowledge that he has a fear; second, to understand that fear is normal and that it's O.K. to be afraid; and third, to overcome his fear through small steps.

If Paul begins to respond to his fear of the lake by exploring it, the underlying fear will probably take care of itself.

Coping with a dreaded object gives a child a valuable lesson in coping with the underlying fear. Such actions also give a child a sense of power that will help him or her to respond to other fears he or she may be confronted with later in life.

Eddie and the thunderstorms provide another good illustration. In helping him, his parents' objective should be to get Eddie to understand thunderstorms and to learn that they are far less dangerous than they appear to be. Again, knowledge is the key.

If Eddie's underlying problem is fear of the uncontrollable, he will be greatly helped if he can come to grips with the fact that there are indeed things in life that are out of our control; but to fear them is to give them even greater power.

Of course, teaching a child that the universe is not the well-ordered, benevolent place they believe it to be can itself induce trauma. The best response is to show the child that those events or situations that are out of our control are not necessarily dangerous or causes for fear. The sun rising or setting, the need for food and sleep, the changes of the seasons are all things that are beyond our direct control, but are not fearsome. By the same token, thunderstorms can be a source of pleasure and enjoyment, if a watcher is safe and out of harm's way.

You must be patient with your child. Distinguishing between those things that we must accept because we cannot change them, and those that we are able to change through strength of will and effort, is a sign of great maturity. Even adults are always learning which is which.

Another lesson we can learn from the examples in Chapter Two is that communication is of vital importance. Children must be encouraged to talk about their fears with their parents.

Shelley lived with her debilitating fear of the man in the wheelchair for some time before finally communicating it to her mother by accident.

How do we get our children to be more open about their fears? A child is not likely to come to a parent and say, "Gee, Mom, I'm afraid of the dark" or "I'm afraid of the water." That won't usually happen, even in the most open home environments.

One way we can begin to create better communication between parent and child is to convince the child that experiencing fear is normal, that everyone has fears. The best way to do that is for parents to talk about some of their own fears and to explain how those fears were overcome.

If a child truly believes that being afraid is O.K., he or she is likely to be forthcoming in discussing his or her emotional reactions to people and events. The child probably will not make a declaration of fear, but he or she may ask questions about the things he or she fears, or

about the feeling of fear.

If, for example, Shelley understood that her fear was relatively normal, she might ask her mother about the man in the wheelchair: Who is he? What happened to him?

It would be natural for her mother to ask why Shelley was interested in him, and Shelley might respond by saying, "Oh, I don't know. He kind of makes me feel creepy."

Her mother's response at this point is important. While she can't be expected to be a mind reader, she ought to be aware that Shelley is, in a sense, asking for help. "Creepy? In what way, honey?" the mother could ask.

If Shelley is open in her communication and not

self-conscious about her fears, she may admit something close to her real feelings: "He scares me a little, and I don't know why." Now parent and child have something concrete to talk about.

If you are attempting to talk to your child about some fear that he or she suffers from, keep in mind that you don't have to play the psychologist. It isn't necessary for you to find the hidden meanings in a child's fear. Be specific and concrete.

Once a child has admitted that his or her fear exists, understands that it is a normal feeling, and makes the decision to overcome it, you can begin to help the child confront the fear. You will then have the opportunity to desensitize the child to that fear, constantly providing support and love.

Identifying the appropriate steps to take is not difficult. Here's an example: Laura, who was six, was spending a week with her parents at an ocean beach. Laura was new to the ocean and wasn't familiar with the strength of the waves as they broke onto the shore.

On her second day at the beach, she was playing at the water's edge when a big wave caught her. Laura went completely underwater and was washed up on the sand where her horrified mother picked her up. It was an understandably frightening experience for both of them.

Laura's parents did their best to comfort her. However, her experience made her fearful of the ocean. She would sit in the sand with her pail and shovel, but wouldn't go near the water.

Her parents encouraged her to talk about her experience. They learned from her comments that it was not the force of the water that frightened her as much as the deafening sound of the wave as it engulfed her. Her parents decided on a step-by-step approach to desensitizing Laura's fear. They first took Laura to a small cove nearby. There the ocean was calmer, and Laura soon adapted to the water again.

Once she was comfortable there, Laura's parents suggested going back to the beach. Laura didn't seem upset at the prospect. Her parents encouraged Laura to play at the water's edge, giving her all the assurance and comforting she needed. This time, she was armed not only with her previous experience but also with her parents' warning to watch carefully for strong waves. Before long, Laura played happily in the water.

This process requires patience and understanding from the parents, and genuine desire to overcome the fear and cooperation from the child, but it works.

Chapter 4

How Do I Begin Discussing Fears With My Children?

Obviously, you're not going to sit your child down and say, "Okay, let's talk about fears." There are many subtle opportunities to discuss the subject if you pay attention to what your child says. This book offers plenty of opportunities to initiate a discussion. Day-to-day communication between parent and child will create others.

The objects of his or her fears can be fascinating for a child, or for anyone. That phenomenon has kept the film industry alive. Consider the number of classic movies that have catered to the public's taste for horror: *King Kong, Jaws, The Exorcist*, etc.

Psychiatric professionals have identified literally hundreds of objects and circumstances that create fear in enough people to warrant special labels, marking them as phobias. There are people who fear elevators, escalators, tall buildings, open spaces, places where there are crowds of people, places where there are no people, string, envelopes, sewing needles, sharp knives, bright lights, insects, and electric utility poles. You name it and there is someone, somewhere, who gets at least a little queasy at it.

You can play a little game with your child that will help him or her become aware that fears are normal. You don't need special circumstances. If, for example, you

are working in the kitchen and conversing with your child, you might say, "Sometimes I'm afraid of sharp knives." It's a common fear. Explain further: "I guess I'm afraid that I might get cut."

Ask your child to name an object that he or she fears. The child might say something like, "Spiders, yuck!" You might respond, "Well, that's not unusual. A lot of people are afraid of spiders. Why do you think so many people are afraid of them? Most spiders aren't dangerous." The child might say, "They're just creepy-crawly!" To which you might respond, "I guess there are a lot of things people are afraid of without really knowing why."

You can take the game a step further by identifying some larger, mysterious fear of your own. "I'm a little afraid of elevators. I feel funny every time I get in one. I think I'm just afraid of small enclosed spaces, and a lot of other people are, too."

You can then ask the child, "What's another thing

that makes you feel a little afraid?" The whole point of this game is to help make the child aware that fears are common to all of us and that confessing to a fear is not itself something to be feared.

Once you have identified a fear or the object of a fear, ask why someone would be afraid of it. The point here is to help the child identify the basis for his or her fear, to help him or her understand that there is always a reason for fear. Children don't necessarily make that connection on their own.

It is difficult for a child to recognize that fear always has some basis, even if that basis doesn't make sense. If a child starts to think of fear in terms of a specific cause, he can begin to come to grips with his own fears. The child now may be inclined to seek answers for this mysterious feeling he has, and may turn to his parents for help in coping with his reactions.

A parent's sensitivity is vital in helping a child cope with his fears. Sensitivity, reassurance, and communication are the three key ingredients in helping children confront and overcome fear.

The importance of physical comforting—the hug, the warm embrace, the strong arm around the shoulder —cannot be overemphasized. When something causes a child to be afraid, physical contact with a parent or another trusted adult has a calming, therapeutic effect on the child.

Understanding that fear is a normal emotion is a critical second step. If parents show children that it's O.K. to be afraid, children will respond in kind.

The importance of communication—open, two-way communication between parent and child—speaks for itself.

Chapter 5

The following pages contain stories about children and their fears. They are intended to be read aloud, and will help your child understand that it is O.K. to be afraid and that it is good for a child to talk about his or her fears with his or her parents.

Though you may recognize your child's own fears in some of the stories, we suggest that you do not single out only those stories to read to your child. The child may remark on this himself, and you can then broaden the discussion, but the main purpose of these stories is to teach your child that fear of one kind or another is absolutely normal.

Depending upon the age and interests of your child, you may want to read only a few stories at a time. You may also find it valuable to engage your child in a discussion of each story. What did he or she think of the story? Did your child find the fear expressed in the story to be unusual or surprising? Does your child ever feel the way the subject of the story did?

This will give you an opportunity to discuss specific fears and the normalcy of fear in general. It also gives you an opportunity to talk about fears that you yourself had as a child and how they affected you.

Keep in mind that the underlying purpose of these stories is to stimulate communication between you and your child.

DORIS'S STORY

Doris was in the kitchen one day, helping her mother with the cooking. Doris enjoyed it. She was nine and hoped one day to be a real chef. Her mom said to her, "Doris, I need a very sharp knife. Will you please reach into the drawer and get me one?"

Doris opened the drawer, but instead of reaching for a knife, she stepped back suddenly. Her mom said, "Doris, what's the matter?"

Doris said, "Oh, nothing, Mom. I was just scared for a second. There's a sharp knife in the drawer with the blade sticking straight up."

Lionel, Doris's older brother, had heard what she said. "If you're going to be a chef, Doris, you can't be afraid of knives," he said.

Their mom said, "What's wrong with being afraid of knives, Lionel? Many people are a little bit afraid of knives, and I'm sure that includes some great chefs. Being afraid of something that's dangerous is

normal. And it keeps you from getting careless."

Doris said, "That makes me feel a lot better. I thought maybe there was something wrong with me, Mom."

"Heavens, no," her mom said. "It's the most natural thing in the world."

Do sharp knives ever make you feel afraid?

ITO'S STORY

Ito was eight and was in the second grade. He was small for his age, and a couple of boys in his class picked on him. Ito didn't fight back. Instead, he just avoided those boys whenever he could.

But their teasing bothered Ito very much, and he felt bad for being afraid of them. He also felt bad about not fighting back, but his dad had told him that nothing is ever gained by fighting.

One day he told his dad how he felt. "I'd like to take a swing at them, Dad. I really would."

His dad said, "Well, Ito, I think that might make things even worse. You're not as big as they are, and they might gang up on you. So I don't think fighting is the answer. The best thing you can do is ignore them and stay with your friends."

Ito said, "They make me feel like a coward. I want to show them I'm tough."

His dad said, "Ito, there is nothing wrong with feeling afraid of those boys. They are very unkind to you and they are

bullies. But maybe you can show them how brave you are by doing something that frightens them but doesn't frighten you."

Ito thought about it for a moment. "You know, Dad," he said, "I've never seen them at the top of the jungle gym, and that doesn't bother me at all."

The next day, Ito climbed straight to the top of the jungle gym, with everyone watching, including the bullies. And after that, they left Ito alone. Ito learned that there was more than one way to face a fear.

Have you ever wanted to stand up to someone who was scaring you?

LUCINDA'S STORY

Lucinda was seven. She was very frightened by thunder and lightning, but she never said anything to her mom and dad about it. She thought they'd say she was being silly.

One night when Lucinda was in bed, there was a terrible thunder storm. Lucinda was so scared that she crawled under her bed and pulled the blanket down with her. In a few minutes her mom came into Lucinda's room to see if she was all right and found Lucinda under the bed.

"What's wrong, Lucinda?" her mom asked. "Do the thunder and lightning frighten you so much?"

Lucinda admitted that they did. She said thunder and lightning always made her very frightened.

Her mom put her arms around Lucinda and gave her a big, warm hug. She said, "Lucinda, there is nothing wrong about being afraid of something. Everybody is afraid of something, sometimes. When something frightens you, you should come to me or your dad and tell us how you feel. We can help you when you feel afraid."

Lucinda said, "Won't that bother you, Mom?"

Her mom said, "Oh, no, Lucinda. You're the most important thing in the world to me. Anytime you feel frightened about anything, you come to me. I'm going to stay right here with you until the storm passes. I won't go away."

Do you tell your parents when something frightens you?

KEVIN'S STORY

Kevin was eleven and he loved baseball. He played on his local Little League team and he was a terrific outfielder. He prided himself on being able to catch anything that was hit near him. His hitting was only average, so he asked his dad for help with it. His dad had been a pretty good baseball player in his day.

His dad worked with him a little and said he thought Kevin was standing too far away from the plate. Kevin said, "Yeah, I know, Dad. But I'm a little afraid of being hit with the baseball. I know I shouldn't be, but I am, and I don't know what to do about it."

His dad said, "Kevin, it's O.K. to be afraid of the baseball. Every ball player is a little afraid of being hit while at bat. It does happen once in a while, so it's a natural fear. Even Major Leaguers feel that way—even I felt that way."

Kevin said, "You did? I thought it was just me."

His dad said, "Not at all. Now let's see if we can get you into a stance that moves you a little closer to the plate and is still comfortable for you."

Kevin said, "Thanks, Dad. You know, I feel better already. I'm glad I mentioned it to you."

Have you ever tried to become more accustomed to something you're afraid of?

JANICE'S STORY

Janice was nine and she loved to go shopping with her mom. Every time her mom went to the shopping mall, Janice would go with her. She liked wandering up and down the store aisles and looking at all the different things that were for sale.

One day Janice and her mom went shopping in a big department store downtown. Janice had never been in such a big store before. It had six floors full of clothes and furniture and other things. Janice's mom said, "We have to go to the sixth floor first. Let's take the elevator."

When they got on the elevator, Janice felt funny. Her heart started beating very fast and her face got all red. She told her mom how she felt.

Her mom said, "I think probably you're a little afraid of being in a small enclosed space. But you don't have to worry, because I am right here with you and the trip is very short." She leaned down and gave Janice a big hug, and by the time her mom had finished hugging Janice, they had reached the sixth floor.

When they got off the elevator, Janice breathed a sigh of relief. "Gee, that was a strange feeling," she said.

Her mom said, "A lot of people are afraid of elevators. But you don't have to be. If you want, we can take the escalator down. Or we can take the elevator one or two floors at a time, or only part of the way."

Janice said, "I think I should try the elevator again—but only for one floor and only if you hold my hand!'' Janice and her mom both laughed a little.

Janice's mom told Janice she was proud of Janice, and they went to do their shopping.

Have you ever tried to do something you were afraid of?

CARL'S STORY

Carl was six and liked just about everything his friends liked—except dogs. Carl was afraid of dogs. He didn't understand why, because dogs had never done anything bad to him.

His friend Johnny loved dogs. Johnny would walk up to almost any dog he saw and pet him and play with him. But Carl always hung back.

Sometimes Johnny would say, "What's the matter, Carl? Don't you like dogs?"

Carl would always just shake his head no. He didn't want to admit that dogs scared him.

One day Carl was walking past the house of a neighbor, Mr. Perkins. He had two big golden retrievers. Suddenly, one of the dogs came running after Carl. He was just being friendly, but Carl was scared and ran away. The dog thought he was playing and kept chasing him.

Mr. Perkins ran after both of them. After he caught the dog, he apologized to Carl and asked, "Are you afraid of dogs, Carl?" Carl was embarrassed, but he admitted that he was.

"That's not unusual," Mr. Perkins said. "I know a lot of people who are afraid of dogs."

"You do?" said Carl. He was surprised. He thought he was the only person in the world who was afraid of dogs.

"Oh, sure," Mr. Perkins said. "Everybody's afraid of something. Some people take to dogs. Some people don't. But you can learn not to be so afraid. I'll hold Goldie very still and you can pet him a little, if you want. He won't bite you, I promise."

Carl wasn't very sure about this, but since Mr. Perkins was so understanding, he decided to pet Goldie. The dog's fur was soft and warm, and he looked at Carl with big, friendly brown eyes.

Carl thanked Mr. Perkins and walked home. He was still afraid of dogs, but not as much as before. Maybe Mr. Perkins would let him pet Goldie again sometime, when he was feeling brave.

Do dogs frighten you? What about cats, or horses?

KIM'S STORY

Kim is eight years old and lives with her older brother and her parents in an apartment building in New York City. Her dad is the superintendent of the building. That means he's in charge of making sure that all the tenants are happy and the building is clean and safe.

One night as the family was sitting down to dinner, the phone rang. Kim's dad went to answer it. He listened for a few minutes and then, it seemed to Kim, he just exploded into a rage and started yell-

ing at whoever was on the other end of the line. Kim was very frightened. She had never seen her dad so angry and she was afraid that he would yell at her like that. She got up from the dinner table and ran to her room.

When her dad finally got off the phone, Kim's mom said, "What was that all about?"

"The guy who was supposed to deliver the plaster never showed up this afternoon, and now he calls up with a lousy excuse and says he can't come at all until sometime next week. That's no good. I need to get this job finished."

"Gee, Dad," said Kim's brother, "you were really mad. I think you scared Kim."

Kim's dad went straight to her room. When Kim heard him coming, she thought he was going to yell at her like he had at the man on the phone. She tried to make herself very small, under her blankets. But her dad just sat down next to her and talked to her in his normal voice.

"Kim," her dad said, "I'm so sorry I scared you like that."

"You really made me afraid, Dad," Kim said. "Why did you yell like that? It was horrible."

"Kim, I just lost my temper. I didn't have any patience left. I know it's scary to hear someone yelling and screaming. I

sometimes scare myself when I get that angry."

"Would you ever yell at me like that, Dad?" asked Kim.

"Believe it or not, Kim, that's something I can't promise you. But I'll always remember that it scares you, and I'll try to remember not to yell at you. That's the best I can do."

"I guess that's O.K.," Kim said. "I promise not to do anything that would make you yell at me."

"That's a deal, baby." Kim's dad gave her a big hug. "Now let's go finish dinner, O.K.?"

"O.K.!"

Do your parents ever do things that scare you?

BOBBY'S STORY

Bobby was six years old and an only child. His dad had died when he was three, and his mom never remarried. She worked full-time, and Mrs. Schmidt took care of Bobby in the afternoons until his mom came home.

One day Bobby's mom said, "Bobby, guess what? I have to go to Chicago tomorrow and stay over there tomorrow night. I'll come home the very next day. Mrs. Schmidt said she'd love to come stay with you while I'm away. How does that sound to you?"

"I don't like it, Mom," Bobby said. He was very upset. "Why do you have to go? Why can't they send someone else?"

"There isn't anyone else to send. This is my project, and I'm the only one who knows what needs to be done. This trip is important to me and to my job." Bobby's mom put her arms around him. "I know that you're worried about being left alone, but Mrs. Schmidt will be here to take care of you."

"What if you don't come back?"
Bobby said. "What if you forget me while
you're away?"

"Bobby, I could never, ever forget
you. I love you." Bobby's mom gave him
another hug. "I know that you're afraid
that I'll never come back because of your
dad, and I want you to know that I understand. But you have to understand, too.
I've never been away from you before, and
I'm a little afraid about it myself."

"You are?" Bobby asked.

"I'm going to miss you very much. I'm going to wonder what you're doing, what you're eating, if Mrs. Schmidt is taking good care of you." Then Bobby's mother had an idea. "Bobby, why don't I call you from Chicago? That way we'll both know that everything is O.K."

"Can you do that, Mom?" asked Bobby.

"Of course I can," his mom said. "And when I get home on Friday, we'll have all afternoon and all weekend to be together." And she hugged Bobby again.

Bobby hugged her back. Bobby's mom helped him mark the days of her trip on a calendar and explained that Mrs. Schmidt would sleep on the couch, not in the bedroom. Bobby started to feel better and told his mom so.

"I'm glad that you're not so frightened anymore. I love you so much. Nothing could make me leave you for a long time. Overnight is long enough, and I will always come back to you."

"Nothing could make me leave you either, Mom!" Bobby said.

"Well, that makes me feel much better, Bobby," his mom said.

"I love you, Mom."

"I love you, too, sweetheart."

Are you ever afraid that your parents will go away and never come back?

JONETTE'S STORY

Jonette is seven. Her mom and dad bought her a bike for her seventh birthday, but she hasn't ridden it in weeks. Jonette fell off the bike a few weeks ago and cut her elbow and her knee. Now she's afraid of bike riding.

One evening her dad asked her, "Jonette, how is your bike? Are you enjoying it?" Jonette said she was.

Her mom said, "I haven't seen you ride in weeks, ever since you fell and hurt yourself. Are you sure everything is all right?"

Jonette didn't want to say anything. She felt ashamed of being afraid to ride the bike. Her dad could tell something was wrong. He said, "Did falling off the bike scare you that much?"

Jonette nodded. She said, "I'm afraid I'll fall again. I'm sorry, Dad. I know you and Mom spent a lot of money to buy that bike for me."

Her dad said, "Jonette, it's O.K. to be afraid of falling off your bike. You hurt yourself pretty badly that time, and it's natural for you to be a little afraid. I don't want you to be embarrassed about any of your feelings. Being afraid is a normal feeling."

Her mom said, "Jonette, would you ride your bike again if your dad and I took you out and gave you a few more lessons?"

Jonette smiled and said, "O.K.—if I can take it easy and just do it for a little while at first."

Her dad said, "It's a deal. Now, where is that bike? It's been out of action for a while. We'd better make sure it's in good working order before you take it back outside."

Have you ever faced up to something you were afraid of?

JIMMY'S STORY

Jimmy was six and in the first grade. He was late for school. He had walked almost to the school crossing before he remembered that he had left his homework in his room. He ran home and got it, and ran back, but by the time he got to school, it was too late. The bell had rung, and everyone was in class.

Jimmy didn't know what to do. He didn't want to go into his class late, be-

cause he knew his teacher, Mr. Madden, would be angry with him, and he didn't know what to say to him.

He sneaked into the school and down into the basement, where he thought no one would see him.

But a teacher did see him. After asking Jimmy where he belonged, the teacher walked with him to Mr. Madden's classroom.

When Mr. Madden saw him, he said, "Thank goodness. There you are, Jimmy. We were all worried about you. Where have you been?"

Jimmy blurted out the story of what happened and told Mr. Madden why he was hiding. Mr. Madden said, "Jimmy, you were afraid that I would be mad at you

for being late—and I was, but I was much more worried that something might have happened to you. It's not good to be late for school, but you made it worse by not coming straight to me and telling me why you were late. You should have just come and told me what was wrong.

"Now go to your seat. I'm not going to punish you, because you are already frightened and worried. You haven't missed anything important." He turned to the whole class. "Let's start that reading game now."

Jimmy felt very relieved. He realized that the best thing to do is to face his fears immediately. The longer it takes, and the more you worry about it, the harder it becomes.

Have you ever been afraid of someone's reaction when you did something wrong?

RUBY'S STORY

Ruby was seven. Once when she was five, Ruby and her mom went to a big department store. Ruby got separated from her mom in the crowd, and it was almost an hour before they found each other again. In the two years since then, Ruby had refused to go shopping with her mom.

Now Ruby was about to start the first grade. Her mom told her that they had to go shopping for some new clothes. Ruby said she didn't want to go. "Can't you do it without me?" she asked.

Ruby's mom said, "You have to come so you can try on some dresses. I can't bring them back here for you."

Ruby was very upset. Her mom said, "Ruby, I know you're afraid because you got lost in the department store a couple of years ago. I promise you I'll keep a close watch on you. I understand that you're afraid. That last time must have been very frightening. But I love you very

much and I will never let anything bad happen to you."

Ruby said, "I'm still going to be a little scared, Mom."

Her mom said, "Yes, I understand that, Ruby. I'm sure that nothing will happen, but if it does, you know what to do, don't you?"

Ruby said that she did. "I should go to the nearest cashier and tell that person that I'm lost. Then they'll find you and bring you to me."

"That's right, Ruby," her mom said.

Have you ever been lost? Were you scared?

ANDY'S STORY

One day Andy, who was six, went walking in the woods with some of his friends. A black snake crawled across the path just ahead of them. When Andy saw it, he got so frightened he turned and ran away.

Andy's friends teased him about it all the way home. That night, Andy had a nightmare about snakes chasing him. He

yelled out loud in his sleep. That brought his dad running to Andy's room.

When Andy's dad got him calmed down, he asked Andy what had frightened him. Andy told him about the snake he had seen, and about his bad dream. He also told his dad that he was ashamed of the way he'd acted in front of his friends.

His dad said, "Andy, there's no reason to feel ashamed about being afraid. Everybody is afraid of something. Lots of people are afraid of snakes. That's normal. Your friends were probably frightened, too. You were just the first one to show it, so they teased you."

"Really?" said Andy. "You mean it's O.K. to be afraid, Dad?"

"Of course," said his dad. "We're all afraid of things we don't understand. If you understood snakes a little better, you'd feel less frightened about them. Why don't we get some books on snakes and look at them together? Then we'll take a trip to the zoo. They have a great collection of snakes. We can look at them up close with no danger. Many of them are actually beautiful creatures."

Andy said, "You mean if you're afraid of something, it helps to understand it?"

"Absolutely," said his dad. "A lot of fears that people have are because they don't understand the things they're afraid of."

Andy thought that was interesting. He looked forward to learning more about snakes. Maybe he could teach his friends a few things about them.

Do you try to learn about the things that frighten you?

KAREN'S STORY

One weekend when Karen was eight, her dad took Karen and her younger brother, Billy, for a holiday at a big lake in the mountains. Karen had been really looking forward to it, but when she saw the lake, she felt a little strange. It was deep and dark, and it frightened her.

Karen's dad rented a rowboat. He was planning to take Karen and Billy for a boat ride across the lake. Karen felt so frightened she didn't want to get in the boat. Karen didn't know why she felt that way, and this made her feel a little ashamed.

Her dad noticed her reaction. "Is the boat scaring you, Karen?" he asked.

Karen didn't want to say anything, but finally, she just blurted out her feelings. She felt so bad she was almost crying.

Her dad said, "Karen, it's all right. Everybody is afraid of something once in a while. You don't have to feel bad, because this is a normal feeling.

"Will you be all right on the shore? I'll take Billy out for a little ride, and when we come back, we'll do something you like."

Karen said that would be fine with her. She felt a little better because of what her dad said. If everybody was afraid of something once in a while, then she was entitled to be afraid sometimes, too.

Have you ever been afraid of a new place?

JERRY'S STORY

Jerry often helped his dad around the house. He was eight, and he was proud that he could help his dad. Together, they'd fix a fence, or straighten a drainpipe, or replace a broken window.

One thing Jerry didn't like was cutting wood. The sight and sound of his dad's

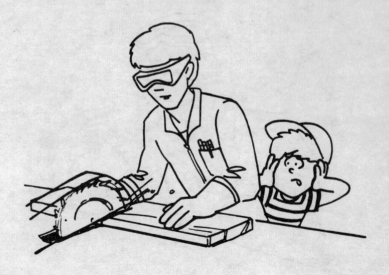

power saw really bothered him and made him very uncomfortable. Jerry would never admit it to his dad, but he was afraid of the power saw.

One day when Jerry was holding a piece of wood for his dad to cut, he closed his eyes very tight when his dad started the saw. His dad noticed, and he said, "This makes you feel funny, doesn't it? I feel that way, too. I guess we're both a little afraid of power saws."

Jerry was surprised. He asked, "Does it really scare you, too?"

His dad said, "Oh, yes. The noise bothers me, and the smell of the engine. What bothers you?"

Jerry said, "The noise, mostly. Sometimes I worry about what would happen if the saw slipped while you were cutting."

"I would never cut you," said his dad. "I'm always careful with the saw. In a way, I'm glad you're a little afraid of this thing. If you weren't, you might get a little careless, and then you might get hurt. A little fear gives you a sense of respect for dangerous equipment. That's the best protection in the world. Men who work well with dangerous equipment usually fear it a little bit. That just makes sense."

Jerry was surprised to learn that fear can be a useful thing if it helps us to be careful around objects that can harm us, and he felt better about his fear of the power saw.

Is there a piece of equipment in your house that you are afraid of?

MARIA'S STORY

Maria was seven. She was just starting to take piano lessons from Mrs. Greer. Maria had been looking forward to learning to play a musical instrument. Her older brother, Tommy, played the guitar and she loved listening to him.

But Maria had a problem. She was afraid of Mrs. Greer, and it was very difficult for her to relax and concentrate on her lessons.

Her mother noticed that something was wrong when she got Maria ready for her third lesson. Maria didn't want to go. Her mother asked her what was wrong.

Maria told her about being afraid of Mrs. Greer. "She's so strict," Maria said, "that she scares me. And I don't think she likes me."

Her mother said, "Mrs. Greer seems strict to you, so you can't tell if she likes you. I'm sure that she does. At the lesson today, tell Mrs. Greer how you feel. See what happens. If you're still afraid after a few more lessons, we'll find another teacher for you."

Before her lesson, Maria told Mrs. Greer how she felt. Mrs. Greer was surprised. She said, "Oh, Maria, are you afraid of me? I'm so sorry. I don't mean to be stern, but sometimes I forget. I like you very much, and I want to work with you. Let's see if we can't become friends."

Mrs. Greer was nicer to Maria after they talked. Soon Maria liked her a lot and had almost forgotten that she had ever been afraid. Piano lessons were fun.

Maria decided her mother was right. Sometimes it's good to tell people how you feel.

Has a person ever made you feel afraid?

KWAN'S STORY

Kwan and some of his friends were playing on the roof of Kwan's apartment building one day. Kwan was nine and liked to be on the roof, where he could see the big blue sky and the boats on the river many blocks away.

Kwan's friend Davey said, "Hey, let's climb over to the roof next door." Kwan was O.K. until he looked down. There was a narrow opening between the two build-

ings, and it was six stories straight down. Kwan stopped climbing and stepped back onto his own roof.

Davey started teasing him. "Come on, Kwan. Are you scared? It's safe. You can step right over the space between the buildings." Kwan wouldn't do it. Davey teased him a little more, but Kwan wouldn't move. When Davey wouldn't come back, Kwan went home.

He told his big brother, Luang, what had happened. Kwan said, "I really felt silly, Luang, but it made me scared to look down."

Luang said, "You felt silly because Davey was teasing you. It's O.K. that you were afraid, because what Davey did is dangerous. You did the sensible thing. There's nothing wrong with being afraid of something. You're afraid of heights. I'm afraid of swimming in deep water. Everybody is afraid of something. What's the big deal?"

"Yes," Kwan said, "but I hate to have someone tease me about being afraid of something."

Luang said, "Let them tease. What's important is that you understand that it's O.K. to be afraid and that everyone is afraid of something, including the people who tease you."

Kwan said, "Thanks, Luang, that makes me feel better. I'll remember what you said."

Have you ever been afraid to do something that you thought was dangerous?

SARAH'S STORY

Sarah was ten years old and an only child. That meant she had no brothers or sisters. But she did have a mom and dad who loved her very much and wanted her to be happy. The family had just moved from their farm to a new town, partly because Sarah's dad had a new job and partly so that Sarah could be around kids her own age.

"Sarah," said her mother one after-noon, "you got some mail today!"

"Is it from Grandma?" Sarah asked.

"No, dear, it's not from Grandma. It looks like it's from that little girl who lives down the street, Martha Tyson. Remem-ber when we met the Tysons after church last Sunday?"

Sarah ripped the envelope open. "It's an invitation to a birthday party, Mom. Martha's going to be ten years old on Saturday." Sarah looked at the invitation for a moment. "I don't think I want to go."

"Why not, honey? It'll be a good way for you to meet some of the kids who live around here," said Sarah's dad.

"I don't know, Dad. I'll have to think about it," Sarah said. "I'm afraid. I'm afraid that they won't like me, or that maybe I'll wear the wrong clothes or do the wrong thing. It just seems easier not to go."

"It's normal to be a little afraid when you have to meet new people. But Martha wouldn't have invited you if she didn't want you to come and didn't think her friends would like you. Even if you're worried, if you go, you'll probably find that you'll have a good time."

"Well, maybe," Sarah said, "but . . ."

"This might help, Sarah," said her mom. "Do you remember your eighth

birthday party? It came just a few weeks after the Amblers had moved in down the road, and we invited Katy Ambler to the party so she could meet everybody? She was probably scared about that, but she came."

"Katy did seem sort of shy at first, I remember. But she's so nice and friendly nobody could help but like her," Sarah said.

"Aren't you every bit as nice and friendly as Katy?" asked her dad, giving Sarah a hug.

"I sure am!" Sarah said. "O.K., I'll go. Maybe I'll get to play with Martha before Saturday and find out what sort of present she wants."

"Good for you, Sarah," her mom said.

Have you ever been afraid to meet new people or do new things?

JOSHUA'S STORY

Joshua was seven and lived in a big old house in the city. He liked the house, especially the big attic, where he could set up his toy trains and let them run from one room to another.

Joshua wouldn't go in the basement. It was very dark, and there were a lot of strange little rooms down there. Once Joshua thought he heard strange noises coming from the basement, even though

he knew that no one was using that part of the house.

One day his mom asked him to go down to the basement and get a wrench from his dad's tool case. It was a dark, gray day. Even with the lights on, the basement was very gloomy. Joshua was frightened. He opened the door to the basement and started to go down, but then he thought he heard something moving down there.

His mom called to him, "Joshua, what's taking you so long?"

Joshua said, "I'm scared to go down there, Mom. I'm sorry."

His mom came to the door of the basement and said, "You are? Well, don't apologize. Sometimes the basement gives me the creeps, too."

Joshua said, "It does? You mean sometimes it scares you, too, Mom?" Joshua was amazed.

"Sure," his mom said. "I know it doesn't make sense, but yes, it scares me to go down there sometimes. I tell myself I'm being silly, but that doesn't change the way I feel."

Joshua felt a little better about being scared of the basement. He said, "Why don't we go down there together, Mom? We can keep each other company."

When they got the wrench his mom needed and came back upstairs, Joshua said, "I thought grown-ups weren't afraid of silly things like that."

"Are you kidding?" said his mom. "Lots of grown-ups still tiptoe past graveyards. Don't you feel bad about being afraid of silly things. I guess it's normal for all of us, no matter what our age."

Are you sometimes afraid of something you think is silly?

SUSIE'S STORY

Susie was eleven years old and had been invited to a slumber party. She was very excited, and when the big day came, she was packed and ready to go hours ahead of time.

Finally, Susie's dad said, "O.K. kiddo, time to go. Let's get all this stuff into the car and I'll take you to Kelly's house."

"I'm so excited, Dad," Susie said. "Kelly's been talking all week long about some surprise she has planned for tonight. I can't wait to find out what it is."

When they got to Kelly's house, Susie's dad said, "Have a great time, kiddo. I'll be here to pick you up tomorrow morning."

The next morning Susie met her dad out by the curb. When she climbed into the car, her dad said, "Well, I can see you didn't get a wink of sleep last night. I guess you had a lot of fun."

"Not really, Dad. I didn't get a wink of sleep because I had nightmares all night long."

"Gee, Susie, you haven't had night-mares since you were a little kid. What do you think brought them on?"

"I know exactly what brought them on, Dad. Kelly's surprise was a tape of a movie called *Attack of the Mutant Frogs*. It was the most scary and disgusting thing I've ever seen. A couple of times I was so scared I covered my eyes—a little too late."

"If it was such a scary movie, why did you keep watching it?"

"Everybody else was watching, Dad. I would've felt like a chicken if I'd left."

"I guess it was hard to leave, even though you were scared. But sometimes

scary movies are less scary if you keep telling yourself that everything that's happening is fake. Remember when we saw that TV show on special effects?"

"Yes," Susie said. "It was neat, seeing how they did all that stuff."

"Well, next time you watch a scary movie, try to figure out how they did the special effects. Sometimes it's easy to guess how, and then you might not get so scared."

"That's a good idea, Dad, but I think I'll stay away from scary movies for a while."

Have you ever been frightened by a movie?

OWEN'S STORY

Owen came home one evening after a school outing at an amusement park. Owen was eleven and in the fifth grade. "Well, how was your day at the park?" his mom asked when he got home.

"Oh, it was all right, Mom," Owen said. "I enjoyed it."

His mom said, "That's not a very enthusiastic reaction, Owen. Is something bothering you?"

Owen said, "Well, Mom, there's a ride

at the park called The Whip. It's a big machine that looks like an octopus. It swings you up and down, and around and around. All the kids wanted to ride on it, except me. It kind of scared me. The other kids all teased me about it and I really felt embarrassed about being afraid."

His mom said, "Owen, it's perfectly natural to feel embarrassed when the other kids tease you. But everyone is afraid of something—even your friends. It's normal. If you had gotten on that ride just because the kids teased you, you probably wouldn't have enjoyed it much."

"I might have gotten sick," Owen said.

"You went to the park to have fun,"

his mom said. "Feeling sick on some ride doesn't make much sense."

Owen said, "But the kids were teasing me, Mom. What could I say?"

His mom said, "You could have told them the truth—that you were frightened. I'll bet there were some other kids who felt the same way, but got on anyway. Owen, there's nothing wrong in admitting to being afraid. Sometimes it takes more courage to do that than it does to go along because you think someone might tease you."

Owen said, "Thanks, Mom. I feel better now that we've talked about it."

Would you have told your friends that you were afraid?

LISA'S STORY

Lisa is eleven years old and just started baby-sitting to earn a little pocket money. She liked to baby-sit, although she'd only done it a couple of times. It seemed like easy money and she liked kids, so that wasn't any problem.

One morning at breakfast, Lisa's mom said, "How did it go last night, Lisa? That was your fourth time baby-sitting. You're getting to be a real pro."

"Some pro," said Lisa. "I don't know if I'll ever baby-sit again."

"Why not? Did something happen last night?" asked Lisa's mom.

"Nothing happened. That's exactly the problem," Lisa groaned.

"Do you want to tell me about it, Lisa?" asked her mom.

Lisa said, "After I had put the kids to bed I sat down on the couch to do my homework. All of a sudden I heard these really strange noises coming from the basement. I swear, Mom, it sounded like there was somebody down there."

"What did you do, Lisa?" asked her mom.

"I went as quietly as I could to the basement door and made sure it was locked. Then I crept upstairs and went into the kids' room and just sat there listening. Mom, I've never been so afraid in all my life. I don't think I moved once until the Shaws got home."

"And then what?" asked Lisa's mom.

"This is probably the worst part," Lisa said. "As soon as I heard them walk in, I ran downstairs and told them I thought somebody was in the basement. Mr. Shaw kind of laughed and opened the basement door, and out walked their cat, Charlie. I could've screamed."

"Oh, Lisa, this is the kind of story

you're going to laugh about in a few days, believe me. But I'm puzzled about your not wanting to baby-sit anymore. It sounds to me like you did just the right thing."

"Maybe I did, Mom. But don't you think that it was wrong of me to be afraid? I mean, I'm in charge and if I turn into a scared little kid all the time, I'm not going to make a very good baby-sitter, am I?"

"Lisa, when people feel afraid of something, it's because their bodies and brains are telling them to be careful and think. Let me see if I can figure out how best to explain this. It's like being afraid of fire, or cars. There's nothing wrong with being a little afraid of them because they can hurt you. Well, when you're baby-sitting, you have to worry about yourself and the kids you're in charge of."

"I get it, Mom. Because I'm in charge I have to be a little extra aware of things that could hurt us—just like I was extra aware of the noises last night!"

"That's right, Lisa. You were right to be afraid, in a sense, because you had a responsibility to protect those kids."

"I feel a whole lot better, Mom. At least I know I wasn't being a baby about it."

"Lisa, I think you acted very grown-up last night. A strange noise in a strange house is very scary indeed, and by going to be with the kids you did the right thing. I hope there was a phone in the room. You do know to call 911 in an emergency, right?"

"Oh, Mom, guess what? I brought the portable phone in with me. I guess I'm the best baby-sitter in the whole world!"

"Hmmm," said her mom with a chuckle. "I see we had no problem getting your self-confidence back—and I'm glad."

Have you ever gotten scared when you were out baby-sitting? What did you do?

PHILIP'S STORY

Philip was seven, and he was having trouble sleeping at night. When everyone was in bed and the house was very quiet, Philip began to imagine things. Sometimes the stairs would creak. Sometimes the wind would make funny noises at his bedroom window. Philip thought that there were monsters all around him, and he was frightened.

He didn't want to say anything to his mom and dad, because he thought they wouldn't understand. Then one night Philip was sound asleep and there was a loud noise at his window. He woke up and was so frightened that he jumped out of bed and ran to the living room, where his parents were watching television.

Philip's mom put her arm around him. "What frightened you, honey?" she asked.

"There's a monster in my room. It was growling at me—it was going to eat me!" Philip was very upset, and his mom hugged him.

"A monster?" said Philip's dad. "Or a noise?"

"A terrible noise," Philip said.

"Let's go look for it together," said his dad. He took Philip's hand, and they walked back to Philip's room together.

Philip turned on the light. Everything looked normal. Then he heard the monster noise again. Philip saw that it was the sound of the wind rattling the venetian blinds. He felt a little silly, being frightened by a sound, but his dad said, "Everyone is afraid of something, sometimes. It's O.K. to be afraid, especially when you can't see what's around you."

Philip's dad closed the window so that the wind couldn't make the noise again. "Anytime something frightens you, Philip, you come and tell me about it."

"O.K., Dad," Philip said. He felt better because his dad had helped him figure out what was frightening him.

When you are afraid, do you try to figure out why? Do you tell your parents when you feel afraid?

YOLANDA'S STORY

Yolanda was seven and in the first grade. She liked school, but there was something about going to school and going back home that Yolanda didn't like. One of the crossing guards frightened Yolanda because he was a great big man who looked scary to her.

So Yolanda started walking the long

way to and from school, to avoid crossing the street where the scary man was. One day when she came home from school, her mom asked her what she had been doing all the way over on Center Street. Mrs. Vasquez had seen her crossing the street there.

Yolanda told her mom why she took the long way home. "That man really scares me, Mom. I feel bad about it, but I can't help it."

Her mom said, "Yolanda, that's all right. The man frightens you and that's O.K. Why don't we try doing something about it? I'll walk to school with you tomorrow, and we'll go past the scary crossing guard together. Is that O.K. with you?" Yolanda said it was.

The next morning when Yolanda and her mom got to the corner where the scary crossing guard was, her mom said, "Why don't we meet your crossing guard?" Yolanda was a little worried, but she felt safe because her mom was there.

"Good morning," her mom said. "This is my daughter Yolanda. She's in the first grade. What is your name, sir?"

The man smiled and said, "My name is Mr. Sandford. Hello, Yolanda. It's nice to meet you." He gently shook Yolanda's hand.

Yolanda and her mom crossed the street and walked toward the school. Her mom said, "Well, I must say he does look a little scary. But once you meet him, he seems nice. What do you think, Yolanda?"

Yolanda said, "Mr. Sandford seems pretty nice to me, too, Mom. I feel a whole lot better about him."

Have you ever faced up to something you were afraid of?

MARCUS'S STORY

Marcus, who was ten, was a big, strong kid. One of the other kids in the neighborhood once described Marcus as fearless, and he was proud of that. But Marcus knew that he wasn't completely fearless.

One day Marcus was playing ball with his friends. Someone hit the ball over the fence and into the backyard of a house next to the park. Marcus went to get it. When he didn't come back right away, his friends went to help him.

Marcus was looking under the back porch of the house. His friend Joseph said, "What's the matter, Marcus, can't you find the ball?"

Marcus said, "I know where it is. It's under there." He pointed to the porch. Joseph asked why he didn't reach in and get it. Marcus didn't say anything and didn't move, so one of the other kids crawled under the porch and got the ball. When he came out, he said, "There are a lot of spiders under there. Marcus must be afraid of spiders. I guess you're not so fearless after all, Marcus."

Marcus felt embarrassed. He told his dad about it that evening.

His dad laughed and said, "So you're afraid of spiders. So what?"

Marcus said it made him feel bad to be afraid of such tiny little things.

His dad said, "Lots of people are afraid of spiders, Marcus. It's not unusual. Everybody is afraid of something. Anyone who says he's not afraid of anything isn't telling the truth."

Marcus said, "You're right, Dad. Maybe I was just trying to fool myself. Spiders just give me the creeps."

His dad said, "Marcus, did I ever tell you about some of the things that frighten me? I've got some real interesting ones for you."

Have you ever asked your parents what they're afraid of?

DEBBIE'S STORY

Debbie was six, and she had a big day ahead of her. In just a few days she was going to start first grade. Debbie had been to kindergarten, but this was different. This was real school.

Debbie's mom was helping her get ready for the big day. They bought new clothes, and notebooks and pencils and a special school bag for Debbie's new books.

As the big day came closer, Debbie got more and more nervous about it. Her mom noticed the change in her mood. She said, "Debbie, you seem to be acting strangely. Is anything bothering you?"

Debbie said, "No, I'm all right, Mom." She didn't want to tell her mom that she was afraid of going to school.

Her mom said, "Now, Debbie, I know something is wrong. Won't you please tell me about it? I might be able to help."

Debbie felt strange about telling her mom what she was thinking, but finally

she did. "This may sound stupid, Mom, but I feel scared about going to school," Debbie said.

Her mom said, "Oh, Debbie, that isn't stupid at all. It's normal. We all feel a little afraid when we start something new. You'll be in a new building, with new teachers, and you'll be meeting new friends. Just think of the excitement of starting something new. And some of the kids in your class will be old friends you'll be seeing again. By the end of the first day, you'll feel very comfortable in school."

What her mom said made Debbie feel better. On the first day of school, she was a little nervous, but she got over it very quickly. Her mom was right. By the end of the day, school felt like something she had been doing for a long time.

Does it frighten you to start something new?

JORGE'S STORY

    One night a sudden bolt of lightning and a loud clap of thunder woke Jorge. He was nine, and he was very frightened. His dad came to his room to comfort him.

    His dad said, "Jorge, did the lightning and thunder frighten you? They scared me, too. It was so sudden." Jorge was so frightened he was shaking.

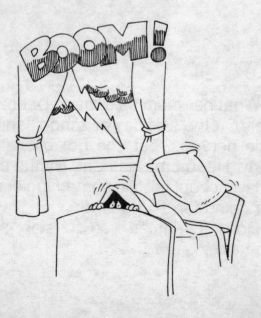

"I thought it was the end of the world, Dad," he said. "I really thought the Russians dropped the bomb. When I woke up, I thought I was going to be dead any second."

His dad said, "Do you worry about the bomb a lot, Jorge?"

Jorge nodded yes.

"I keep thinking that I'll never get a chance to grow up," he said.

His dad said, "That's perfectly understandable, Jorge. It's a very frightening thing for all of us."

"Do you think it could happen, Dad?" Jorge asked.

"It could happen, Jorge," his dad said, "but I don't think it will. I have just one reason for that, but it's the best reason anyone could have. I love you, and I want you to grow up and enjoy life. Russian fathers love their children just as much as I love you, and they don't want it to happen either. As long as there are children in the world, and parents who love them, I think we'll find a way to keep from blowing ourselves up."

Jorge said, "I hope when I grow up, kids won't have to worry about the bomb."

His dad said, "I hope so, too. If we're lucky, maybe your generation will find a way to rid the world of that terrible danger. In the meantime, love is our protection, and that's as good a protection as we can hope for. Now give me a big hug, and let's see if we can get back to sleep."

What frightens you the most?